Prayers for a New Generation

A Confirmation Keepsake

by

JOSEPH MOORE

Paulist Press

New York / Mahwah

Book design by Nighthawk Design

Copyright © 1991 by
Joseph Moore

All rights reserved.

Library of Congress Cataloging-in-Publication Data

Moore, Joseph, 1944–
   Prayers for a new generation/by Joseph Moore.
      p. cm.
   ISBN 0-8091-3246-X
   1. Teenagers—Prayer-books and devotions—English.   I. Title.
BV4850.M66   1991
242'.83—dc20   91-21397
                                                                      CIP

Published by Paulist Press
997 Macarthur Blvd.
Mahwah, N.J. 07430

Printed and bound in the
United States of America

Prayers for Gifts of the Spirit

PRAYERS FOR WISDOM

Make me wise and shrewd, O God
In a world of vipers and deceit
Where others' values tug at me
And pull me down to places I don't want to go.

Bring me up and boost my spirit, Jesus
And make me wise so I can see what's going on
So I can recognize manipulation
And call it by its name and thereby
Make it powerless over me.

* * *

Dear God,
So often I don't know
How to act,
What to say,
Who to listen to,
Which to choose
Where to go or
How long to wait.

Give me wisdom so I can act
And not be paralyzed
So that I can move out in confidence
In a confusing world
Knowing that you are by my side
Guiding me.

PRAYERS FOR UNDERSTANDING

Dearest Lord I pray that you
Can help me understand my parents
And that I by them may also be,
Understood.
So often we argue, so often we hurt
Each other, we don't mean to but we do.

They grew up at another time and don't seem to accept
That this is a new world we live in
Help them know it has nothing to do with my
feelings for them.

Help them to understand that I want to be me
To live my own life, to make my own choices.
Help me to tell them it's time to let go
To set me free
Without hurting them, without making them
Think I have no appreciation for all they have done.

Help us to understand each other, dear Lord.

Amen.

* * *

Help me to understand, Jesus
People who think different
talk different
look different
value different
pray different
from me.
Help me to appreciate that life is a mosaic of
differences and that differences are good.
Keep me from thinking that everyone else
Should be just like me.

* * *

I don't understand my best friend.
I thought I knew her inside out.
I thought we could tell each other anything.
I thought we both wanted to be best friends forever.

But now she's changing.
Or maybe it's me, I just don't know.
But I always expected that life would be the same
Inside the white picket fence of our childhood.

But now we're growing apart which makes
me feel angry sometimes, and sometimes
hurt and sometimes sad.

I wish that things didn't have to change
I wish I could hang on to some things forever.
I wish I could understand life a lot more.
I wish I still knew my best friend.

PRAYERS FOR KNOWLEDGE

Let me know the cool breeze of your Spirit over me
Let me know the gentle warmth of your Love within me
Let me know your presence in the stillness of my soul
Let me know, just let me know
That, Jesus, you are here.

Help me on the dark days when it seems you've gone away.
Help me on the sunny days when you are here to stay.
Let me know, just let me know
That, Jesus, you are here.

* * *

Dear God above it seems that I
Had yet another crossroad nigh.
Again a choice before me lay
Help me, dear God, to know the way.

Because I don't know what to do
I turn my thoughts once more to you.
And stretch to you my shaking hand
That you might bring this ship to land.

* * *

Help me in school to concentrate
Help me to study, help me to learn.
Give me the knowledge I'll need in my life.
Give me the patience and self-discipline.
Teach me to listen, teach me to write.
Teach me to challenge and teach me to care.
Keep me from wasting my talents and gifts.
Keep me from failing my folks and myself.
Help me in school when I tune it all out.
Help me in school, God, please help me in school.

PRAYERS FOR COUNSEL

HUMBLE ME, GOD
I always think I know it all
Even though I know I don't
Deep down that is.
It's hard for me when someone else corrects me
Or gives advice, chastises me and
Says that I am out of line.
I want to strike right back
And say "well who are you?"
"What right have you to tell me what to do?"
But then I know humility
Is such a gift
To listen to the counsel of my family, my friends.

I wish that I could do that
Please humble me. Amen.

* * *

Spirit of God,
Enlighten me
Grace of God,
move me
Heart of God,
electrify me
Compassion of God,
touch me
Hand of God, heal me
Passion of God,
stir me
Mind of God,
Counsel me.

PRAYERS FOR PIETY

Two men went up to the temple to pray.
One was a rich man, the other a stray.
The first one was glad about all his good deeds.
The second felt empty and gave God his needs.

Not lifting his eyes he begged God for grace.
The rich man considered him just a disgrace.
Yet God only smiled on the poor man that day.
Who raises the low and sends rich on their way.

* * *

Teach me to pray
In simplicity of heart
Teach me to stay
When I want to run away
Teach me to quiet down
All my anxious thoughts
Teach me to stay around
When I want to flee
Teach me to pray, O Lord
Teach me to pray.

* * *

As evening falls and shadows tumble
gently over weariness
I lift my hands, I stop and stumble
My words are few, my thoughts are less.

Take my prayer so weak, so feeble
As I lay my body down
Let my raised eyes be the steeple
Heart beats like the hymns resound.

PRAYERS FOR FORTITUDE

Stay here and keep watch with me
Watch and pray . . .

Stay here and keep watch with me
Watch and pray . . .

Jesus, I feel so weak so often
Like your friends who fell asleep
When you asked them just to be nearby
To watch with you and pray.

Give me strength when I'm alone
And no one stays with me.
Or when I feel like quitting, Lord
And leaving you behind.

Stay with me, keep watch with me
Watch and pray.

* * *

The road is narrow
Winding, steep
Like a sparrow
Without sleep
Jesus walks
to Calvary,
Jesus walks
to Calvary.

Teach me narrow
Ways to walk
Like a sparrow
Without talk
Behind Jesus

up the hill
Behind Jesus
Silent still.

Stretch me out
Oh Crucified
Be the solace
At my side
Jesus, friend
Who died for me
Jesus, nailed
Against a tree.

When life knocks me
To the ground
Tell me, Jesus
You're around
Walking with me
Up that hill
Like a sparrow,
Silent, still.

* * *

Sometimes I feel I can't go on
Sometimes I feel so forlorn
Sometimes I feel like I want to cry
And sometimes I feel like I want to die.

Then is when I turn to prayer
Then I give God my every care

Then I give Jesus all of my pain
Then I get sunlight after the rain.

PRAYERS FOR FEAR
OF THE LORD

Jesus the lover
You accept me unconditionally
I can never stray too far.
But you are also my challenger, Jesus.
Calling me always to greatness
Inviting me to share more,
to give more
to trust more
to pray more
to be more.
Let me never forget that you call me
Call me to be uncomfortable
with the status quo within myself
And also in society.
Challenge me, Jesus to
ever grow.

* * *

When I lay me down to sleep
Childhood angels at my feet
Then I think that life will end

Jesus be my faithful friend.

In the daylight death seems far
But at dark I see a star.
Then the thoughts will reappear
of passing time and holy fear.

Jesus, help me spend my days
In the choosing of your ways
Matthew, Mark and Luke and John
Bless the bed that I lie on.

Prayers for Fruits of the Spirit

PRAYERS FOR CHARITY

Dear God,
I don't always feel like being nice
Sometimes I'm just so irritable and
People bug me for no reason at all.
I'm moody too and take it out on those
Who won't reject me . . . my family and friends.
Help me to get a grip on my emotions
When I feel like being nasty.

"Love is patient, love is kind
Love's not jealous, never rude
Not self-seeking, never broods
It's not snobbish . . . love is kind."
      (A paraphrase of 1 Corinthians 13:4–5)

* * *

Sometimes I walk a city street
And see a man with dirty feet
Sitting in a doorway.

I want to stare but look away
For fear that he will want to say
He needs some change from me.

I don't know what it is I feel
Some pity for the lousy deal
He got in living life.

Or maybe guilt is more what I
Feel as I pass him quickly by
That I don't stop to help.

Help me God forget myself
I'm like a doll upon a shelf
I do not get involved.

Expand my heart with charity
That I might see with clarity
There but for grace go I.

PRAYERS FOR JOY

Gratify, satisfy
Words that I use
Drugging and partying
Brain cells abused!

Help me get over
The crazy idea
That happiness dwells
In a bottle of beer.

Lead me to peacefulness
Rivers of joy
Help me grow into a man from a boy.

* * *

Dear Jesus,
When I talk with you at twilight
A deep joy comes over me
And all my problems shrink in size.

Help me to share the joy you give me
In my family where I can be such a grouch
With my friends where I can be so depressing
At my job where I can be such a complainer
With that special person where I can be such a nag
In my school where I can be such a zombie
Within myself where I can be so insecure.

PRAYERS FOR PEACE

I notice there are two kinds of peace . . .
One that's real and one that isn't.
One that comes artificially from drugs or
from nobody speaking the truth or
from avoiding conflicts with people or
from being afraid to say what you really think.
From being afraid to do something others will disapprove.
Help me Jesus, to avoid the pseudo-peace and

To seek the real peace.
A peace that comes from getting my highs in natural ways
A peace that comes from speaking the truth
A peace that comes from less caring about what others
    think
A peace that comes from verbalizing anger
A peace that comes from being myself.

* * *

Black and brown, yellow red and white
There are many colors but why do people fight?

Christian, Moslem, Hindu, Buddhist, and Jew
There are many faiths, can only one be true?

Communist, socialist, capitalist view
Must one be imposed on the others too?

Can we build a world where all differences are banned?
Can't we just be people standing hand in hand?

* * *

When my parents annoy me,
Give me patience, God.
When my teachers badger me,
Give me patience, God.
When my friends upset me,
Give me patience, God.
When my boss offends me,
Give me patience, God.

When I'm mad at myself,
Give me patience, God.

* * *

I live in an instant world, Jesus
Technology has made it so easy, so fast.
We have computers, and airplanes and highways,
Calculators, fax machines and television.
Telephones, Federal Express and automatic tellers.

But every once in a while, technology breaks down
And I find myself having to wait for something
That I'm not used to waiting for.
And I can't handle it because I haven't learned to.
Life is so smooth, so fast for me usually.
But I need to gain patience so I won't get so frustrated
So upset and out of control because I have to wait.
Help my generation to discover patience, Jesus.
It's really hard for us.

PRAYER FOR KINDNESS

It's not easy to be kind.
I don't know how you did it, Jesus!
Sometimes when I read the Gospel
I feel like you weren't human
Like I am.

Didn't people ever bother you?
Crowds all pressing in
Blind and lame and old and babies
I'm sure you had my feelings
They just aren't written down

Help me to be gentle
When I feel like shoving someone
Help me to be silent
When I want to be real mean
Teach me kindness Jesus
I want to be like you.

PRAYER FOR GOODNESS

Help me God to be real good
Doing what I know I should
Letting go of all that's bad
Habits that I've often had.

Let me be your friend anew
Doing what I ought to do.
Speak no evil, do no wrong.
Act like Jesus all day long.
  Amen.

PRAYERS FOR FAITH

When the sky is gray
Help me believe in blue

When the earth is dry
Help me believe in rain.
When the night is long
Help me believe in light
When the tears don't stop
Help me believe in smiles
When my heart feels empty
Help me believe in love.

* * *

"Walk on the water," said Jesus to him.
"I'll keep you buoyant and you won't fall in."
"Trust me, dear Peter, for I'm on your side."
"Just keep on walking and swallow your pride."

Yes, dearest Jesus, I'm often like him.
You say to walk to you, I'd rather swim.
Help me to trust that you'll never let go.
Stretch out your arms to me, keep me in tow!

PRAYER FOR MODESTY

It seems square today to be modest
To play down sex appeal and to present yourself
In a decent, respectful way,
The media is charged with sex
And all the messages it sends invades so many thoughts.
Yet deep within myself I know

I admire a modest person
Who just says, "here I am" with no great airs,
Without pretense or sexual innuendos
But as they are. I admire that.
Help me to be like that too, dear God.
Help me.

Prayers for an Anxious Generation

PRAYER ABOUT DIVORCE

I don't understand
What is going on.
I don't know what to do
I feel like a football
Tossed around a field
I am very sad
I feel all alone
Was it me who caused all this
Or was it not at all
Why are they hurting me
Why can't they just try.
Help me, God, I'm so confused
I don't know where to turn
Help me, God, I'm all alone
With an empty heart.

MASKS

I took a look in the mirror today
Who is the person I see?
Am I the same as yesterday
Where can I find the real me?

I wear so many facades in one day
No one can figure me out.
When I'm with these friends I act in one way.
I'm one way at home and one out.

How can I go on just living these lies
Being so fake, so unreal
Tear from me, God, all the masks I despise
These layers of falsehood to peel.

Let me become that real me that's inside,
With values and thoughts so unique
All the pretensions help me put aside
And let the real me finally speak.

A PRAYER WITH THOUGHTS OF SUICIDE

Dear Lord,
Sometimes I want to end it all
I don't know why
Sometimes I feel I can't go on
My life is such a mess
No happiness in view
No light at the end of my tunnel

Help me to hang on to hope
And choose good friends to talk with
Instead of isolation.
Let me cling to life again
This precious gift you give me.
Give me just a spark of hope
To burn within my heart
Give me just a spark, O Lord
That I might carry on.

PRAYER FOR ADDICTS

I am stuck, God
Stuck like glue
Out of luck, God
Turn to you

"Jones'n" Jesus,
Picking up
Save me Jesus
I'm corrupt

Can't let go, Lord
Can't let go
Higher Power
Your face show

Give me courage
Strength to quit
I'm an addict
Feel unfit

Lift me out, Lord
From the mire
Of addiction
I'm on fire

Sweetest Jesus
Wipe my brow
Sweetest Jesus,
Show me how.

PRAYER FOR CHASTITY

Dear Jesus, Help me to keep myself for that one person
To whom I will want to give
All that I am.

Help me not to fragment myself,
In a desperate search for love and approval
From people who won't commit to me.

Let me know within myself
How much you value me, how worthwhile I am
What a gift I could be to another.

A PRAYER WHEN STRESSED

Stressed out
Pressed down
Feeling bummed out
Want to drown

Nerves are shattered
Let me go
Feeling tattered
I don't know
How to keep
The pressure down
Keep my feet, God
On the ground.

PRAYER ON A DATE

Keep me honest, faithful to
All my values that are true

Give me honor and respect
For my date, my passions checked

Help us not to have a fight
Rather spend a pleasant night

Let us grow in trust and love
Watch us, Jesus, from above

Prayers in Season

AN ADVENT PRAYER
John 14:9

Unadvent me
O Jesus God
And shed away my ripened reddened
leaves of expectation
Stark, let me stand;
flung wide against the white chilled sky
my branches be, and bare
But I am not a tree
a man am I
there is no need to wait upon a Springtime.

He came, He comes, He cometh
was and is
yes in this time and on this place
and with these longing lifted eyes
I tell them "wait upon other Springtimes"
a season yet to come (It never will)
this here and now fall all too harsh on me
("Phillip" call my name)
Don't say that on my shuttered, cluttered porch
stands God this very day
Oh were I but a tree

I'd sooner wait upon a Springtime
Amen. Unadvent me.

A PRAYER IN AUTUMN

I trip
I skip,
And lap the earth,
I flee,
I fall
And mesh
With other leaves
In soggy rains . . .
I slumber
in the dampened dark
The night is mute
and chill
and still I sleep aloof, alone,
Yet one above the twinkling stars,
Warms this November night
and me
with solitary watchfulness.

A WINTER PRAYER

Cold is the night
And I am laughing.
My laughter ripples

In the still nothingness.

Black is the sky
And I am crying.
And no one wipes the tears away
From my stained cheeks.

Oh other people are laughing
And crying too . . .
But they turn around
And don't look at each other
Until their facial contortions have achieved
A compromise.
And their joy is locked
In the gulp of their throats.
And their sorrow is stashed
At the bottom of their hearts.
And they pull the curtains across
Behind their eyes
So no one can look down
And see what all of us know
And do not know.

For only the fool (and the little child)
Can laugh at the sun
And cry out loud in the winter night.

A LENTEN PRAYER

A tree stood strong and full and young
And flung its branches to the sky;

Beneath the tree a flower sprung,
Sown silently nearby.

And all the woodland knew this ark
Whose mighty shadow mocked the sun;
A blossom crept onto the bark,
The tree, the flower, one.

But one dark night a raging gale
Swung up and struck the giant tree,
That fell with shout and distant wail,
For eyes no more to see.

In quiet space the flower stands
Alone to meet the rising dawn,
And with her beauty tells all lands
That flowers do live on.

AN EASTER PRAYER

Mary danced on morning dew
Was this Jesus whom she knew?
Sweetest grass in morning light
Gone the shadows of the night

Run to tell the others now
He is gone, I don't know how
Bid them haste to be with me
Gone ahead to Galilee!

AT PENTECOST

Spirit descending in wind and flame
Flood my soul and call me by name
Give me your strength to preach in his name
To give the blind sight, to set free the lame.

A PRAYER IN ALL SEASONS

Hear us oh great Spirit
Which hovers mightily over the running waters

Spirit that mounts dawn with light to
spill over every dark corner of the earth

Spirit that makes the summer rains to fall
and bathes the soil in tenderness

Spirit that is higher than the icy mountain
peak, and deeper than the swirling sea

Spirit living in ancient wrinkled eyes
and every new born's eye as well

Spirit moving in every heart which
heaves with pain and every heart
which leaps in joy

We thank you, mighty Spirit
Father, mother of all that lives
For all that is

For all that was
For all that will be in unseen tomorrows.
Receive our thanks.

MORNING PRAYER

At break of day I stand before you, Jesus
The darkness that protected me has fled away.
I stand exposed before the sun
Which floods my face for all to see.
Like when I stand before my bathroom mirror
The harsh light scrutinizes all my blemishes.
And that's how this day feels to me
A day to probe my inner self,
To bring dark corners into light
A day to look at myself squarely in the eye.
Where am I going? What's dragging me down?
What are the things I need to change?
These are the questions I have for myself this morning.
I want to walk in the light, today.
I want to be a child of the light.

OUR LADY OF NIGHT

Softly seeps the starlight in,
The blanket of dusk unfurls.
Peppered with angelic dust,

The Milky Way untwirls.

Our Lady descends with the darkness,
Mistress of a starry sea.
And as I look up at twilight to heaven,
I see her smiling at me.

Psalms for Now
(paraphrased)

PSALM 23

The Lord is my friend
And that is all I need
In gentle meadows he gives me rest
He leads me along the calm lake side
And restores my energy
Even if I'm having a bad day
And I can see no light at the end of the tunnel
I never lose hope
For you are with me

PSALM 73

How good God is to those whose hearts are pure
But as for me, I came so close to the edge
Envious of evil doers
Who don't seem plagued by daily troubles
These "fat cats" have just what they want
They even mock God
Why bother to be good?

This is sometimes how I feel
But when I really think about it
I realize how temporary everything is
Why throw away eternity for a moment's pleasure?
God keep me close to you
And save me from slippery ways.

PSALM 121

Shall I look to power,
wealth and fame for help?
No, my help is from God.
He will never let me
stumble or fall because
he always watches over me.
He never sleeps, my defender
He protects us from all evil,
He preserves our lives.
He keeps his eye on you
as you come and go.

PSALM 125

If you trust in the Lord
You will be as steady as a mountain
As hills protect the valley towns
So God surrounds, protects his people

Keeping all the wicked out
Oh Lord do good to those of us
Who try in our lives to be good
Give us security and quiet peace.

PSALM 131

O Lord, my heart isn't proud
Nor do my eyes look down on others
Nor do I busy myself
With things that don't concern me.
Like a baby on its mother's lap
I am relaxed in your arms
Oh Israel, hope in the Lord
Hope in the Lord and be still.

PSALM 133

How wonderful it is,
how pleasant when
brothers and sisters live
in harmony. Harmony is
as precious as expensive
perfume in a world
that is fractured by division.
Harmony is as refreshing
as dew on a mountain top,

an eternal blessing
of the Lord.

PSALM 148

Praise God Oh heavens
Praise him from the skies
Praise him sun and moon
Praise him stars and neon signs
Praise him hail and ice and snow
Praise him skiers as you glide
Mountains, hills and ghettos too
All the poor who labor so
Young and old and in between
Praise the God of Israel.

"DE PROFUNDIS"

Out of the depths
Out of depression
Out of the mire and
Out of the fire
I call to you, O Lord
Hear my pleas
I'm on my knees
Beaten down by enemies
What will become of me
Without thee?

Prayers for Social Justice

THE OLD WOMAN

There's an old lady who sits on the stoop
And her face is crinkly and rosy pink
And her eyes are glazed, yet startling blue
She has by her side all that she owns
In a beat up old duffle bag
Her legs are large with the veins of childbearing
And I wonder if she has a son
I wonder if she has a daughter
And if she does, why they leave her there
To sit and stare in such despair.

FREE SOUTH AFRICA

Blood of children
On the ground
Doesn't someone hear the sound?
Of people crying to be free.

How can I participate
How can my own country wait
When people are not free

How can Christians tolerate
Leaders that prefer debate
To setting people free

We can't have another day
When injustice has its way
People must be free.

PRAYER FOR PREJUDICES

People of color
Various strands
Come to this country
From so many lands

All of us live here
Sharing the earth
No one is better
By race or by birth

Teach us dear Jesus
To open our heart
To one another so
No one's apart

Let fear and let prejudice
Fade and dissolve

To live as a family
Be our resolve.

* * *

AIDS is an illness with many in its web
Help us God to be your people here on earth.
To embrace those whom life has dealt a cruel blow.
To mirror the compassion pouring from your eyes.
To make no judgments either about those
Whose weakness as a person may have given them this
    disease.
Knowing that we too are just as weak as they
In our own way
Give to them and give to us, strength to love today.

JESUS IS

Jesus is in every face.
He is every laugh,
He is every tear.

Jesus is in every heart.
He is at every wedding,
He is present for every funeral.

Jesus is in every soul.
He is in the eyes of the naive young children,
He is in the hurt, the anguish of an abused son.

Jesus is in every mind.
He is a new born baby,
He is a dying friend.

Jesus is in every squeal of joy,
He is in every shriek of terror.
He is felt in every embrace,
He is present in every war.

Jesus is the reason why.

Jesus is the who, the what.

Jesus is.
     (Michael Adams)

A PRAYER FOR RESPECT OF LIFE

We pray today for all unborn
With tiny feet in mother's womb
And ask that we shall never mourn
Life's promise sent into a tomb.

We pray today for all of those
Who although born still have no shoes
Children destitution chose
Their haunting glances can't excuse.

We pray for feet deformed and maimed
By bullets, bombs and senseless war
May peace forever be proclaimed
May bloodshed cease forevermore.

We pray for feet behind steel bars
That walk the concrete prison yard
That they might focus on the stars
And know our care when life is hard.

We pray for feet so strong and black
That suffer from the feet that's white
South Africa do not turn back
We join our spirit in your fight.

We pray for feet confined to bed
In lonely antiseptic rooms
We join our own to tears you've shed
We wait with you 'till Springtime blooms.

We pray for feet grown gnarled and old
By journeying life's weary way
We often leave you in the cold
Forgive our thoughtlessness today.

And Blessed are the feet that bring
The comfort that the Gospel gives
And Jesus' challenges that sting
God's word which nourishes and lives.

Prayers for Appreciation

PRAYER FOR OUR PARENTS

As dark night steals upon my youth,
I turn back to the dawn,
And to the day that it gave birth,
Nearly gone.

As daybreak swathes the newborn sky,
My mother warmed her child;
And like a birdsong thrills the air,
My father smiled.

Like rain that softly nurtures earth,
They bathed me in that hour
With urge and love and laugh and tear,
A gentle shower.

And when the beating mid-day sun
Flung its scorch across the sky,
They hovered me in cool retreat
With tenderness nearby.

Then when it began to sink,
They led me out with love whereon
When twilight spilled the dimming sky
They tarried on.

And now as awesome shadows fall
And gnawing night breaks through,
I plunge alone into the dark,
My path revealed by that one spark
Which trips through air from that one star
That they have hung in God's broad sky
Then stand afar.

EYE OPENER

We have eyes, yet we don't see
the beauty that God has given to us.
Everyone places their values on
the wonders of heaven that God
has promised us.
We need to see the heaven we have
on Earth. The wonders of nature,
beauty of the forest, innocence of
a child, and the good of people
We often forget about the good in
the world, and are blinded by the darkness.
God, please give us all the wisdom to
enjoy the heaven on Earth.
The strength to right the wrongs,

and not turn away.
The will to fill this world with your love.
    (Richard Nunes)

Note: This poem was written by Rick, age 24, from his prison cell, where he is serving time for crimes resulting from drug addiction. He is also dying of AIDS.

Praying the Scriptures

JEREMIAH'S PRAYER

"Lord God," he said, "I am too young."
"I really don't want to be a prophet."
I really don't want to stand up all by myself
To ignore the pressure of those around me
And do the right thing and
Say the right thing
All by myself.

But "fear not, Jeremiah," said the Lord
"Say not, I am too young."
I wish that God's word was just for adults
I wish that kids didn't have to be Christian
I wish I could say "I too am too young"
I wish I didn't have to grow up.

But the Lord answered Jeremiah
"To whomever I send you, you shall go;
Whatever I command you, you shall speak
Have no fear before them,
Because I am with you . . . ."
I guess you're with me too, dear God
Please take away my fear
Please be with me, Amen.

* * *

Gentle Jesus
On my knee
Once again
A child to be
How I wish that I could find
Simplicity of heart and mind
No pretensions, no defense
Recovering my innocence.
Like children, you said, we should be
Full of light and honesty
Help me, Jesus, find a way
To a simpler childhood day.

* * *

Woman,
Where are those that condemn thee?
I'll tell you what people
truly offend me
People who set themselves
way up above
These people don't know
the meaning of love.
Judging their brothers and sisters
they lose sight of the
Gospel they say that they choose

So judge not another,
accept everyone
On good folks and evil
God shines the same sun.

* * *

Martha, Martha
Take a rest
Mary does what
I like best

She just listens
At my feet
Come and join us
Take a seat

Always busy
Working so
Woman, restless
On the go.

Mary chose
the better part
Loving me
With all her heart

Think about
The way you live
Time is but
The gift you give.

* * *

Like the lilies of the field
Let my restless spirit yield
Like the birds that fill the air
Teach me to release my care.
Like the sparrow in the tree
I know you take care of me.
Nothing matters, in the end
Since I have you as my friend.

* * *

Nicodemus came at night
Full of questions, full of fright
Since he was a pharisee
He came out in secrecy
Asked the Lord what he should do
To find life in God anew
Jesus said "to be reborn"
Nicodemus looked forlorn
Jesus then went on to say
This was birth another way
Birth by Spirit, water too
This was what he ought to do.

Help me let go of my fears
When I go against my peers
Jesus' friend by night *and* day
I will walk the narrow way.

WOMAN AT THE WELL

Who are you sir upon the rock?
How is it that you wish to talk?
To me a woman, not your kind
I've left my husband far behind

I've come to draw some water up
Would you like me to fill your cup?
How is it that you know my past?
And speak to me of lowly caste.

What is this water that you give?
Which means that I'll forever live
In that case, Sir please fill my jar
For life is long, the journey far.

A Guided Meditation on John 4:1–33 (paraphrased)

Close your eyes . . . breathe deeply . . . and relax. Stretch out on the floor if you can.

(PAUSE)

It's a hot summer's day and you have decided to go to the well to draw out some cool water. You carry a bucket up a hill to the shade of a small tree near the well.

(PAUSE)

You are surprised to see a man sitting under the tree. He is dozing but your presence awakes him.

(PAUSE)

"Hello," he says with a smile. His eyes are warm and his face is pleasant. "My name is Jesus."

(PAUSE)

"Hello," you reply and tie your bucket to the apparatus to lower it into the well. Your thirst is really getting to you now.

(PAUSE)

"Will you give me a drink? I have no bucket," says Jesus.

(PAUSE)

"Sure." You draw your bucket and pass it to Jesus who gulps down some water like a thirsty man.

(PAUSE)

"Thanks." He passes the bucket back to you and you drink. "Who are you? Tell me about yourself."

(PAUSE)

You feel like resting and talking to this stranger and so you begin to tell him who you are and what is preoccupying your thoughts these days.

(EXTRA LONG PAUSE)

Jesus responds to you. What does he say?

(PAUSE)

You feel better after this conversation. Jesus tells you that while you came to draw water from the well, you will be thirsty again. But he says that he has "water" to give also and that those who drink of this water will have a "spring" inside of them to eternal life.

(Pause and continue your
conversation with Jesus,
bidding him farewell)

A Guided Meditation

I. Introduction: Jesus has something very special to say to each of you. Let's give Him the time to do that right now.

Close your eyes.

Take a deep breath. Inhale (1-2-3-4); Exhale (1-2-3-4).

(Repeat this 10–15 times)

II. Imagine your spirit leaving your body and floating above you, through the roof to the outside above this retreat house (place). It can be any time of day:

The mellow expanse of sunlight at dawn or the sad shades of orange at sunset.

The sky can be bright and blue or gray and stormy or it can be dark and crisp and peppered with a thousand stars.

Choose whichever sky you want, whichever suits your mood and allow your spirit to go soaring through it.

(pause here for one full minute)

III. Travel now in your imagination through your sky, away and away until you come to the favorite place of your childhood, whatever that might be. It could be a tree, or a backyard or a cottage or your grandmother's kitchen. Remember what your favorite place was and maybe still is and *be there* now, all by yourself.

(pause here for one full minute)

IV. Allow Jesus to appear also at your favorite place. He stands before you, takes your hands and looks lovingly into your eyes. In your imagination visit with Jesus now.

(pause here for one full minute)

Jesus calls you by name. . . . (pause briefly) and thanks you for being here today in order to grow in love and in maturity. He asks you how the day is going for you. . . . He asks you about the risks you have taken or not taken today to share your life with other people.

(pause briefly)

He asks you if there is anything you need from Him today to help you in your everyday life. Talk to Jesus now about what you need from Him.

(pause here for one full minute)

Jesus again holds your hands, looks into your eyes and promises that He has heard your need and that He *will* respond and that He *will* help you. And then He tells you it is time for Him to go.

V. You are alone again in your favorite place but you feel differently because of your visit with Jesus. Let your spirit swiftly soar again in your sky, a sky which is the same or perhaps a sky that has changed. Soar in that sky as far back as you came and allow your spirit to reenter these walls and reunite with your body. (pause here). Now open your eyes, slowly.